VOICES IN HIP-HOP

DRAKE

CASEY DW JONES

CREATIVE EDUCATION / CREATIVE PAPERBACKS

...'Cause ever s

city, you

...Starte

goin'

...Glasse

on the

Published by Creative Education and Creative Paperbacks
P.O. Box 227, Mankato, Minnesota 56002
Creative Education and Creative Paperbacks are imprints of The Creative Company
www.thecreativecompany.us

Design by Graham Morgan
Art direction by Blue Design (www.bluedes.com)

Images by Alamy Stock Photo/Sam Kovak, cover, 3, 27; Getty Images/Cole Burston, 39, Ethan Miller, 23, Gilbert Carrasquillo, 9, Harmony Gerber, 31, Ian West - PA Images, 36, John Shearer, 16, Kevin Winter/DCNYRE2011, 19, MARK RALSTON, 35, Noel Vasquez, 25, Paras Griffin, 10, Prince Williams, 2, 40, 46, Raymond Boyd, 15, Ross Gilmore, 44, Steve Granitz, 14; Pexels/James Wheeler, 12; Wikimedia Commons/musicisentropy, 4, The Come Up Show, 28, 43

Library of Congress Cataloging-in-Publication Data
Names: Jones, Casey DW, author.
Title: Drake / by Casey DW Jones.
Description: Mankato, Minnesota : Creative Education and Creative Paperbacks, 2026. | Series: Voices in hip-hop | Includes index. | Audience: Ages 12–15 | Audience: Grades 7–9 | Summary: "Listen up! It's Drake, the versatile and emotional hip-hop artist. Part biography, part song lyric collection, this music-fueled title for high school readers celebrates the rapper's journey and voice. Includes a selected discography and index"– Provided by publisher.
Identifiers: LCCN 2024050296 (print) | LCCN 2024050297 (ebook) | ISBN 9798889892779 (library binding) | ISBN 9781682776438 (paperback) | ISBN 9798889893882 (ebook)
Subjects: LCSH: Drake, 1986– –Juvenile literature. | Rap musicians–Canada–Biography–Juvenile literature.
Classification: LCC ML3930.D73 J65 2026 (print) | LCC ML3930.D73 (ebook) | DDC 782.421649092 [B]–dc23/eng/20241023
LC record available at https://lccn.loc.gov/2024050296
LC ebook record available at https://lccn.loc.gov/2

Printed in India

I might be too strung out on compliments, overdosed on confidence

VOICES IN HIP-HOP / DRAKE

Started not

nce I left the

ng less and

e

ampagne out
floor

OCTOBER'S VERY OWN

contents

• • •

contents

• • •

VOICES IN HIP-HOP

Foreword

• • •

"When Drake's music was brought to me . . . it was about rap, you know, and I was, like, 'This dude sound different.' What I loved about him was that he was sounding just as dope as we were. When I say we, us, I'm talking about the streets . . .

"I told him, 'You literally could make working in the cubicle . . . sound like the dopest thing in the world to do . . . Don't stop. Don't change.' Then one day I heard, '[singing voice].' Like, 'What the f— was that?' . . . I remember asking Mack [Maine], 'Who that is [singing] on the hook?' He's, like, that's him, too. And I'm, like, 'Are you a singer?' And he's, like, 'You know, I mess around' . . . And I said, 'OK, you got to be the ultimate artist.'"

—LIL WAYNE, RAPPER, *I AM ATHLETE* PODCAST, MARCH 7, 2022

Introduction

T wenty years ago, if asked to think about Canada, some Americans might've pictured ice hockey. Others might've pictured a maple leaf, beavers, or the Royal Canadian Mounted Police. All of those national symbols are still valid. But ask any fan of popular music today what they picture when they think of the country up north, and many will say one name: Drake.

The Canadian-born rapper, singer, and songwriter known as Drake is one of the best-selling artists in music history. Since 2006, he has released eight studio albums, one collaborative album, and several other mixtapes and releases. Bringing melodic singing and an R&B feel to hip-hop, he has sold more than 170 million records worldwide. He has appeared on several popular singles with top hip-hop artists such as

Mary J. Blige, Kanye West, Usher, and Lil Wayne. He has even outsold many of the lions of hip-hop, including Jay-Z and Eminem.

In addition to his commercial success, Drake has racked up plenty of awards. He's won eight American Music Awards, several BET and BET Hip-Hop Awards, and dozens of Billboard Awards. He has five Grammy awards, too. In 2021, he received the Billboard Music Award for Artist of the Decade.

Not bad for a kid from working-class Toronto.

Toronto, Canada

Early Life

• • •

Drake was born Aubrey Drake Graham on October 24, 1986, in Toronto, Canada. His father was Dennis Graham, a drummer from Memphis, Tennessee. His mother was Sandra "Sandi" Graham, an English teacher and florist from Toronto. Dennis was African American, and Sandi was an Ashkenazi Jew.

The Grahams divorced when their son was only five years old. Sandi and Drake remained in Toronto, while Dennis returned to Memphis. Dennis spent time in prison for many years of his son's youth for drug-related offenses, which meant he was required to remain in the United States until Drake's early adulthood. Before that time in prison, however, Drake would spend summers with his father in Tennessee.

Drake's uncles on his dad's side are also musical artists. One of them, Larry Graham, was a member of the renowned funk and soul group Sly and the Family Stone. While his father's background in music no doubt played a role in his future musical dreams, Drake always wanted to go a step further than his dad. He wanted to be an icon.

Drake grew up in two Toronto neighborhoods. First, he and his mother lived on Weston Road, in Toronto's working-class West End. He was a talented hockey player, but a nasty hit to his neck cut his career short. At the request of his mother, who feared for her son's safety, Drake gave up the sport. In 2000, they moved to a wealthier neighborhood called Forest Hill.

That n— Memphis for real, girl, he love you to death
He made mistakes throughout his life that he still doesn't accept
But he just want our forgiveness, and f— it, look how we living
I'm content with this story, who are we not to forgive him?

—FROM "YOU & THE 6," ON THE 2015 ALBUM *IF YOU'RE READING THIS IT'S TOO LATE*

School Days

This ain't the son you raised who used to take the Acura
5 a.m. then go and shoot *Degrassi* up on Morningside

—FROM "WORST BEHAVIOR," ON THE 2013 ALBUM *NOTHING WAS THE SAME*

s a child, Drake attended a Jewish day school, where he felt like nobody understood what it was like to be Black and Jewish. Then, when he and his mother moved to the "nicer" side of Toronto, he had even more problems with school. It was tough being a mixed-race kid from the other side of town. He was often bullied.

Drake's mom didn't make much money, but she did the best she could. Growing up in that lean environment shaped Drake's work ethic. He recalls doing his Bar Mitzvah in the basement of an Italian restaurant instead of at the expensive venues where his classmates did theirs. The music video that he later made for "HYFR" was his attempt to do it all over again—this time with money. He also wanted to reconnect with his Jewish neighborhood. But not having as much as everyone else around him inspired Drake to make a name for himself, so he started his own career in entertainment early.

In 2001, at age 14, Drake auditioned for a TV series called *Degrassi: The Next Generation*. It was about a group of kids at a community school who were navigating through the ups and downs of life. Drake was cast in the role of Jimmy Brooks, a basketball star who had become paralyzed from the waist down after being shot.

At age 15, Drake officially dropped out of high school. He was close to graduating, but he felt he needed to make money to help his sick mother. Drake's stint in television ended in 2009, however, when the show's producers discovered he was working on his mixtapes on the side. He had to choose between acting and music, and Drake chose music.

After his rise to the top of the hip-hop and R&B charts, Drake decided to go back to high school. He finished his degree through correspondence courses in 2012.

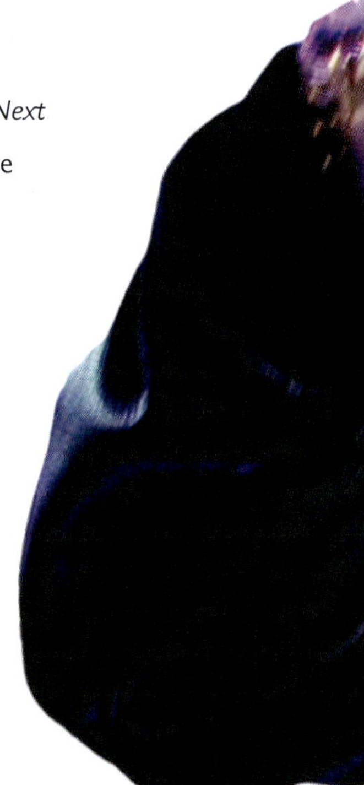

... Baby, you my everything

... You all I ever wanted

... We could do it real big

Drake Arrives

Drake started making mixtapes in 2006, while acting on the set of *Degrassi*. His first one got him some attention in the hip-hop world, with several well-known artists wanting to work with him. In 2007, his brash track "Replacement Girl," featuring Trey Songz, was the Joint of the Day on BET's music video show *106 & Park*. This led to guest appearances on other artists' mixtapes. An up-and-coming Drake was enjoying support from the heavy-hitting likes of Jay-Z, Kanye West, and Lil Wayne.

However, it wasn't until 2009, when Drake released his third mixtape, *So Far Gone*, under his own October's Very Own record label, that he hit it big. Led by the hit single "Best I Ever Had," *So Far Gone* was met with critical and commercial success. The mixtape's release party in Toronto was attended by NBA star LeBron James. The mixtape scored two Grammy award nominations, and Drake signed a major recording contract with Young Money Entertainment.

The public was hungry for more from the young artist. Drake delivered when he dropped his debut studio album, *Thank Me Later,* in 2010. The album was moody and introspective. Many of the songs were about parts of his own life, including love. He hinted about a brief relationship with the Barbadian singer Rihanna. *Thank Me Later* debuted at number one on the Billboard 200 music chart and sold 447,000 copies in its first week. Most music reviewers praised the album. Others said it was too sad-sounding. Some said the tracks didn't sound like they were all part of the same album. But the album made a large cultural impact. Music fans were listening to it and discussing it. And Drake was just getting started.

TAKING A NAME

Drake's stage name comes from his middle name, chosen by his father. The artist isn't sure why his dad picked it, though. He once told *HipHopCanada*, "My dad is a character, so it could be anything. I just really loved the name, and I embraced it my whole life." Although it's his professional name, Drake is also how he's known in everyday, off-stage life. As he said, "Drake is who I am." His other stage names include Champagne Papi, Drizzy, and 6 God. They reflect Drake's diverse cultural and class background.

Something Different

Critics and fans alike loved the atmospheric elements and grooves on 2009's *So Far Gone*. Drake impressed with his ability to make it all blend together. That's always been a huge part of his appeal. *So Far Gone* had a lot of lo-fi elements, including soft piano, horns, and synthesizer melodies. Those elements were in large part thanks to Noah "40" Shebib. When other artists were using auto-tune, Drake and 40 steered clear of it. The *So Far Gone* mixtape wove in and out of a variety of moods. There were upbeat and downbeat R&B samples.

Drake and Noah "40" Shebib

Nothing was off-limits to sample. Drake and 40 used pop, indie rock, and soft rock samples alike, from artists such as Billy Joel, Jay-Z, and Swedish indie rocker Peter Bjorn. Tracks such as "Best I Ever Had" sampled different-sounding songs all in the same track. It was the blending of moods, soft and hard, that made the mixtape stand out from the crowd. Drake and 40 even found a real laid-back groove on "Successful" (featuring Trey Songz and Lil Wayne). It wasn't Drake's first collaboration with either artist, but it was a taste of things to come.

Some people have gone so far as to call Drake's style "Rap&B." He switches from rapping to singing with the snap of a finger. "Best I Ever Had," the song that made Drake's popularity explode, showed just how catchy his songs could be.

And she live in a mindset that I could never move to
Until you find yourself, it's impossible to lose you
Uh, because I never had you although I would be glad to
I'd probably go and tattoo your name on my heart

—FROM "HOUSTONLANTAVEGAS," ON THE 2009 MIXTAPE *SO FAR GONE*

VOICES IN HIP-HOP

The Lonely King

• • •

How an artist deals with fame almost always informs their next big piece of work.

On *Thank Me Later,* Drake's first full studio album, he faced his fame head-on through his lyrics. The album sold more than 80,000 units in Canada in less than a week. The introductory song, "Fireworks," was a celebration of his string of successes—from mixtapes to hit singles to signing a big record label deal. Other lyrics on the album dealt with his fear of success, his newfound celebrity status, and all the gossip that came along with it.

With his second studio album, *Take Care,* the lyrics were highly emotional and dealt with his newfound fame. He was no longer guessing what it would be like to be at the top. He knew. The cover art showed Drake staring into a gold chalice, a lonely king with nobody beside him.

Take Care won the Grammy for Best Rap Album in 2012 and is considered one of Drake's finest works. The tracks connect easily to listeners' ears. At times, it feels like he's reading his diary aloud. The lines between rapping and singing, hip-hop and R&B are even more blurred. The depth and range of this album—everything from club tracks for dancing to soulful love songs—are what sets it apart. Many music experts believe this album is still his best effort. The album showed his willingness to transform himself, and his sound, in order to reach new heights as an artist. A decade later, artists such as Billie Eilish still credit this dark, moody masterpiece as an inspiration.

Let's stay together 'till we're ghosts
I want to witness love, I've never seen it close
Yeah, but I guess I gotta find it
First, that's why I'm really going off
Fireworks!

—FROM "FIREWORKS," ON THE 2010 ALBUM *THANK ME LATER*

The Good and the Bad

• • •

Looking back over Drake's career now, it's easy to see what sparked his appeal. He came from a multicultural family. The city he grew up in was not known as a place for hip-hop music. Drake was not like other hip-hop artists, so he did not feel the need to make his music sound like theirs. He was simply "Drake." Fans loved his unique sound, and he quickly became known as one of the "nice guys" in rap.

Drake mentioned his rising-star status on every mixtape. Each new effort saw a more polished artist. The most important year of his career turned out to be 2009, when *So Far Gone* blew up. That led to his 2010 effort, *Thank Me Later*. Drake's first full studio

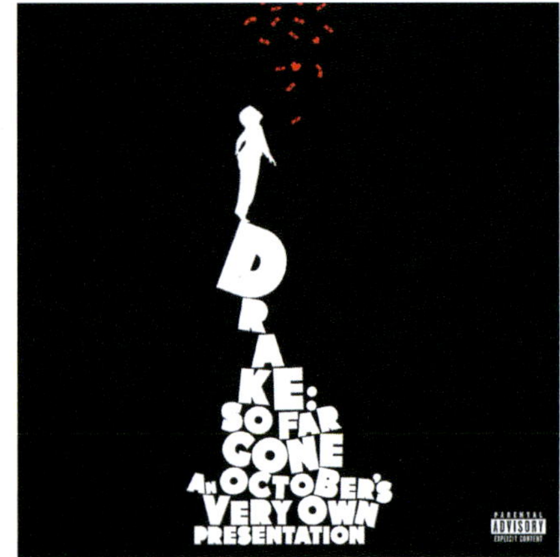

album was one of the most anticipated hip-hop albums of the time and regarded as one of the best of the year. Many people drew comparisons to Kanye West, one of his idols.

From then on, each new album Drake dropped won awards and topped the charts. But as his star rose, it seemed that Drake's ego did, too—a common pitfall of stardom. His earlier nice boy image began to tarnish. By his 2023 album, *For All the Dogs,* Drake encountered controversy. He was accused of misogyny, a hatred of, or prejudice against, women. He took shots at his rumored ex-girlfriend Rihanna, as well as Megan Thee Stallion. Many listeners and critics were turned off by Drake's attacks on the two singers and other Black women of hip-hop and R&B. They held out hope that the artist would rein it in and evolve as a person and as an artist.

TORONTO SOUND

Drake's early mixtapes helped define the "Toronto Sound." The Toronto Sound is typically a little bit slower and more sparse than other rap and R&B. There's more crunch to the bass than boom. On top of that foundation, the Toronto Sound is emotionally intense. It's like creating a void into which an artist can pour their soulful lyrics. Drake's "Days in the East," from the 2019 album *Care Package*, is a good example of the Toronto Sound.

Cover of the 2016 album *Views*

Making Hits

Drake's third studio album, *Nothing Was the Same,* stormed the charts in 2013. In terms of sales, there wasn't much of a drop-off from *Thank Me Later.* The album reached number one on the Billboard 200 and sold more than four million units in the United States. Yet it didn't quite have the staying or selling power of Drake's second studio album. So, Drake went back to work.

After releasing two mixtapes in 2015, including a surprise joint venture with rapper Future, Drake recorded his fourth studio album, *Views*. Released in April 2016, it featured guest appearances from Wizkid, Future, and Rihanna, among others.

Views debuted in the number one-spot on the Billboard 200. By almost every measure, it was the greatest success of Drake's career to date. Within the first week of its release, the album smashed a record by clocking more than 245 million online streams. Each of the album's 20 songs appeared on the Billboard Hot 100, including the widely played singles "One Dance" and "Hotline Bling."

Despite selling more than six million units, *Views* didn't receive as many positive reviews as *Nothing Was the Same*. Some people said the album failed to break enough new ground. In his lyrics, Drake explored romance failures, betrayal, insecurities, and infidelity, while also celebrating deep friendships. In the music, he experimented with different sounds and styles. *Views* is largely informed by West Indian and West African music. The same year it was released, Drake collaborated with Rihanna on the single "Work." This music helped bring dancehall-inspired pop, infused with Jamaican influences, to new audiences.

'Cause ever since I left the city, you
Started wearing less and goin' out more
Glasses of champagne out on the dance floor
Hangin' with some girls I've never seen before

—FROM "HOTLINE BLING," ON THE 2016 ALBUM *VIEWS*

Drake poses with his awards during the 2017 Billboard Music Awards in Las Vegas, Nevada.

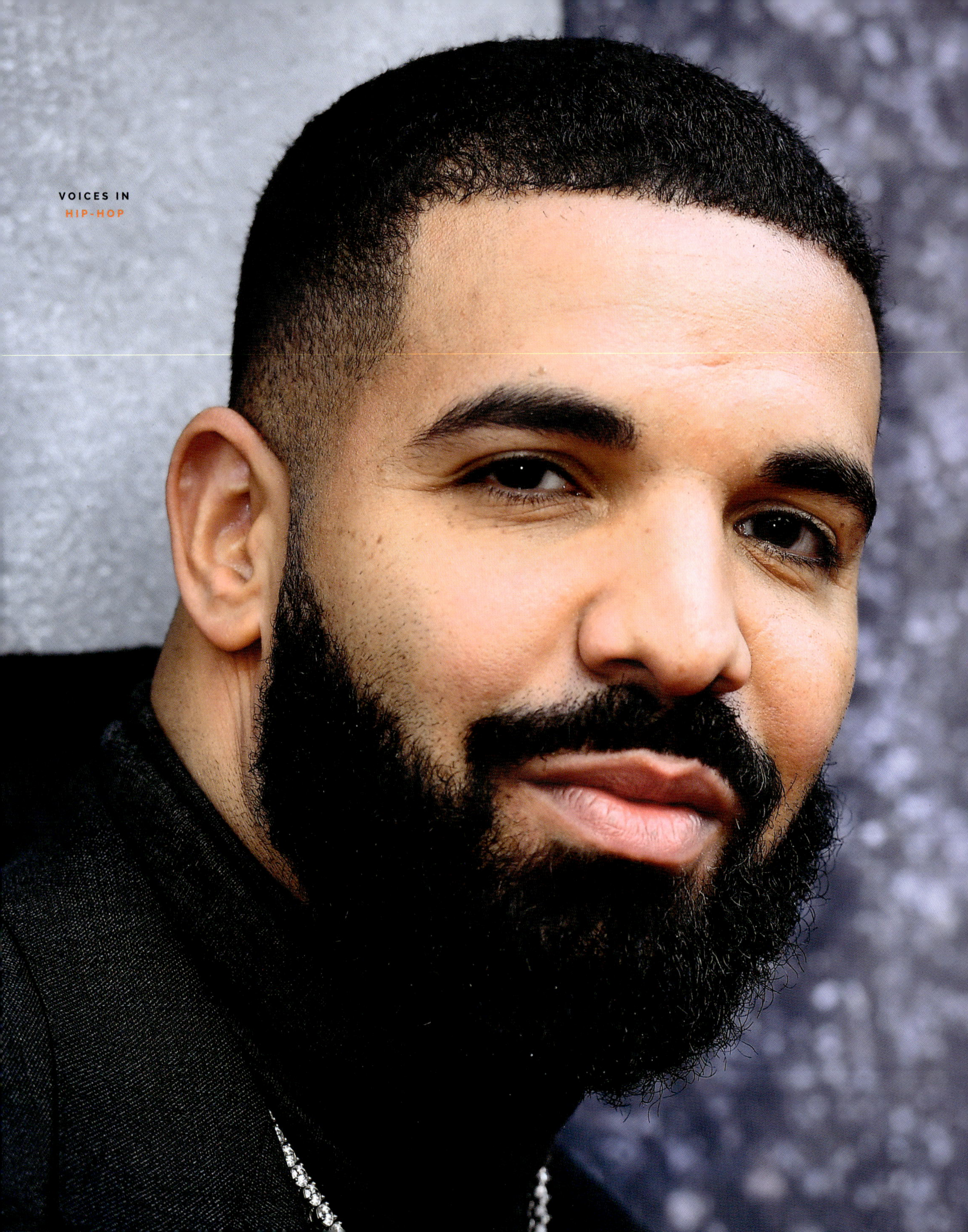

Beyond the Music

• • •

Over the years, Drake has mostly kept his politics private. He prefers to promote peace, love, and harmony through his music. He believes his concerts are a place like his hometown of Toronto, where people celebrate the diversity and cheerful optimism of North America.

In 2016, U.S. presidential candidate Donald Trump appeared on the late-night sketch comedy show *Saturday Night Live*. During the show, Trump did a parody of Drake's "Hotline Bling" video. Drake did not endorse the parody. In fact, he did not have much to say about it at all. However, in 2017, he did seem to take aim at what

he saw as then-president Trump's divisive nature. Drake criticized him in a speech at a London concert.

Drake has received some criticism himself for his lack of social responsibility. He isn't regularly involved with any specific charity organizations, but that doesn't mean he's not charitable. In 2018, he donated nearly the entire $1 million budget for his "God's Plan" music video to people in Miami, Florida. He gave gift cards to a women's shelter. He presented a scholarship check to an unsuspecting student. He paid for everyone's groceries at a supermarket.

The giving behind "God's Plan" shows Drake's approach to charity. He likes it to be a surprise. Recently, Drake hit it big at a casino. With his winnings, he gifted $1 million in Bitcoin to the LeBron James Family Foundation, which creates change in James's hometown of Akron, Ohio.

Now I'm seein' money off of hotlines blingin' but it feels different
Transitions, plans switchin', ambition
Mindin' my business, buildin' a business, etcetera
Inspired by a few, but my mind really drives itself like Tesla

—FROM "DEEP POCKETS," ON THE 2020 MIXTAPE *DARK LANE DEMO TAPES*

Drake and LeBron James

She say, "Do you love me?" I tell her, "Only partly
I only love my bed and my mama, I'm sorry"

—FROM "GOD'S PLAN," ON THE 2018 ALBUM *SCORPION*

Personal Life

Never a matter of could I or should I?
Kiss my son on the forehead then kiss your a— goodbye
As luck would have it, I've settled into my role as the good guy
I guess luck is on your side
I guess luck is on your side

—FROM "8 OUT OF 10," ON THE 2018 ALBUM *SCORPION*

rake lives his life out loud in a lot of ways. It's no secret that he still calls Toronto home. He lives in a $100-million estate called "The Embassy." It's a perfect nickname, considering how seriously he takes his role as a global ambassador for the city of Toronto via its professional basketball team, the Raptors.

... If you thinkin
I'mma quit
before I die,
dream on

... Man, they
treat me like

Drake's never been shy about talking about his love life on his albums. He had a relationship with singer-songwriter SZA between 2008 and 2009 and an on-again, off-again romantic relationship with Rihanna from 2009 to 2016. He even professed his love for Rihanna at the 2016 Video Music Awards, a moment that she called "uncomfortable." She claims they are no longer friends.

One area of his life in which Drake demands more privacy is in his role as a father. He shares a son, Adonis, born October 11, 2017, with French artist Sophie Brussaux. He first denied his relationship to the boy. But he eventually confirmed his fatherhood on his 2018 album *Scorpion*.

Adonis has appeared on a few songs with his dad, and the youngster is already doing some of his own rap performances. Recently, Drake disclosed that Adonis was responsible for the artwork on the 2023 studio album *For All the Dogs*. Even though Drake has said he wants the media to leave his son alone, he doesn't seem shy about pulling him into the spotlight himself. It may be only a matter of time until Adonis's songs are topping the charts like his father's.

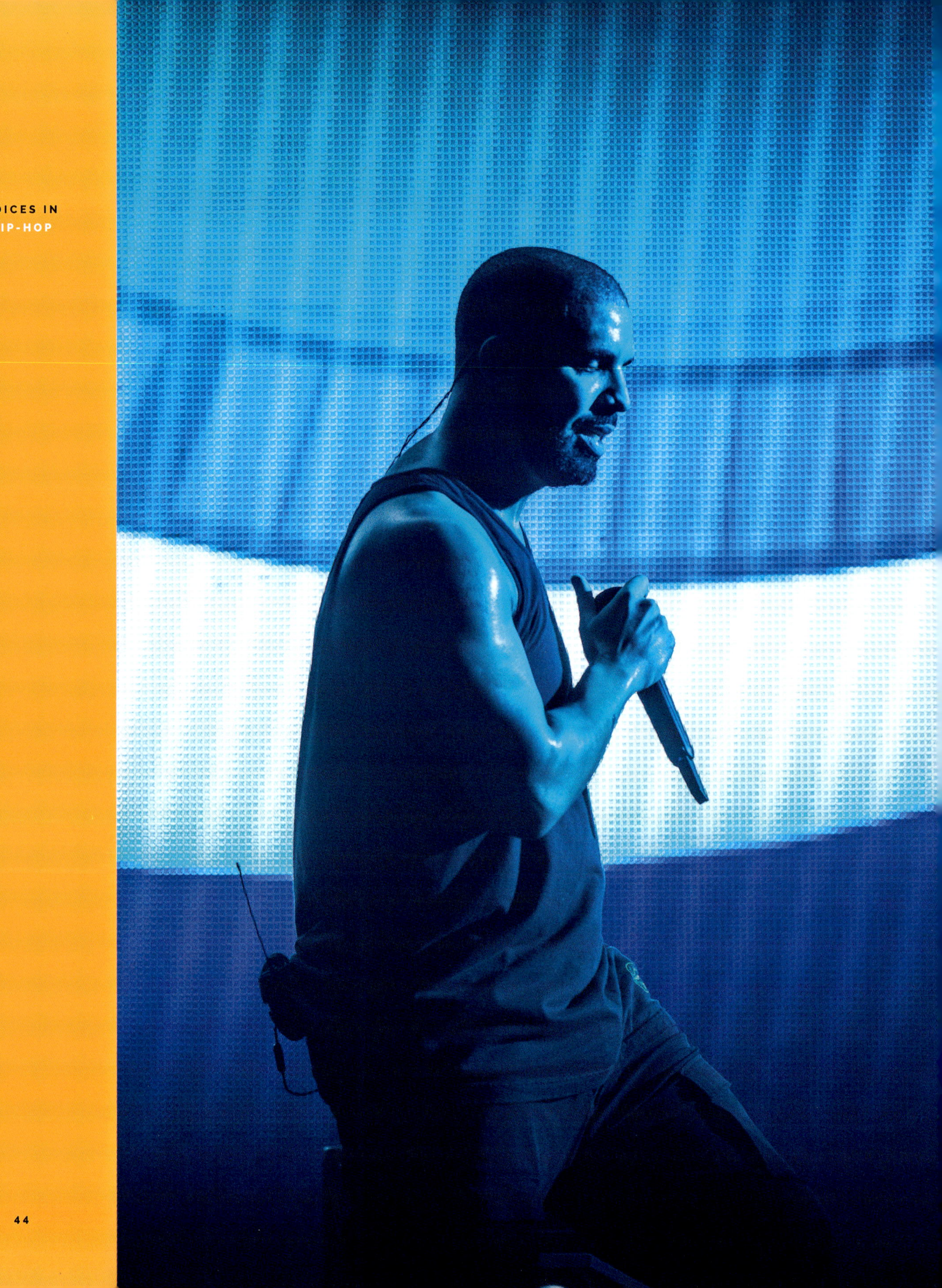

Far from Over

rake set a fast pace for himself after 2016's *Views*. He released his fifth studio album, the wildly successful double album *Scorpion*, in 2018, *Certified Lover Boy* in 2021, and *Honestly, Nevermind* in 2022. His eighth studio album, *For All the Dogs*, came out in 2023 to mixed reviews, with some critics calling it "bloated" and "tiring." They said the mistrust of women in Drake's songs, particularly directed toward Rihanna and Megan Thee Stallion, felt "particularly bitter." However, despite the controversy, *For All the Dogs* marked Drake's 13th number-one album on the Billboard 200.

Drake followed up *For All the Dogs* just a month later with *For All the Dogs Scary Hours Edition*. The deluxe album combined the original set with six new songs. It included more than 10 collaborations with other top artists, such as Bad Bunny, J. Cole, Lil Yachty, and SZA. Tracks were broken up by reports from fictional radio station BARK. Snoop Dogg acted as one of the radio station's DJs during interludes.

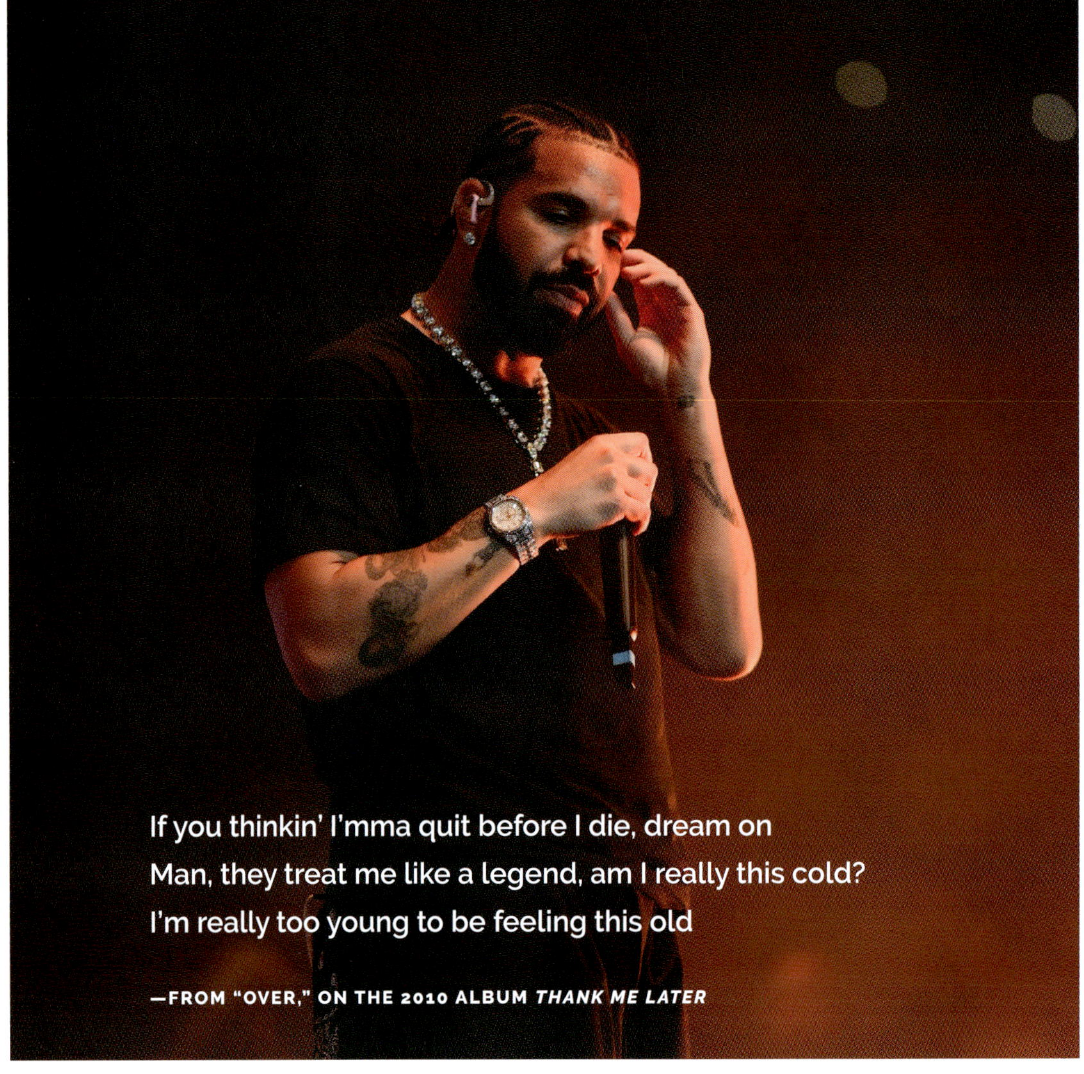

It remains to be seen what long-term effect the criticism will have on Drake's career. Will he mature and apologize for his misogyny? Will he lose his relevance? Will he release another album anytime soon?

On the October 6, 2023, episode of his radio show, *Table for One,* he said he was going to "lock the door on the studio" and take some time to focus on his health and well-being. As for how long fans might have to wait for Drake to return to music, he offered, "maybe a year" or "a little longer." It might be awhile, but one thing is certain: Whenever Drake unlocks that studio door, fans know it'll be well worth the wait.

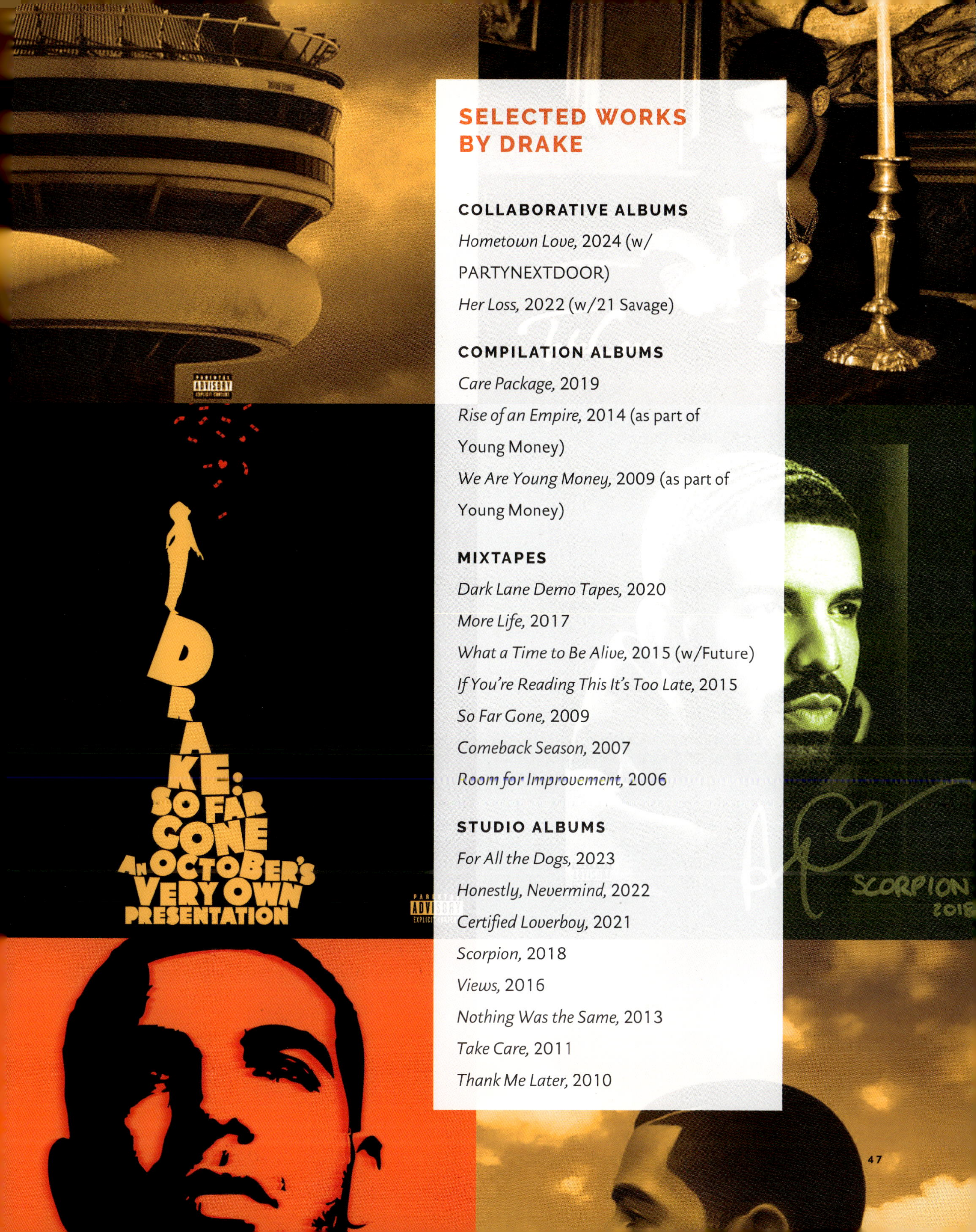

SELECTED WORKS BY DRAKE

COLLABORATIVE ALBUMS

Hometown Love, 2024 (w/ PARTYNEXTDOOR)

Her Loss, 2022 (w/21 Savage)

COMPILATION ALBUMS

Care Package, 2019

Rise of an Empire, 2014 (as part of Young Money)

We Are Young Money, 2009 (as part of Young Money)

MIXTAPES

Dark Lane Demo Tapes, 2020

More Life, 2017

What a Time to Be Alive, 2015 (w/Future)

If You're Reading This It's Too Late, 2015

So Far Gone, 2009

Comeback Season, 2007

Room for Improvement, 2006

STUDIO ALBUMS

For All the Dogs, 2023

Honestly, Nevermind, 2022

Certified Loverboy, 2021

Scorpion, 2018

Views, 2016

Nothing Was the Same, 2013

Take Care, 2011

Thank Me Later, 2010

INDEX